THE PHOTO-LIBF

# *George Reid*

# *Streets of London*

## *in the late Twenties & early Thirties*

### Edited by Mike Seaborne
### Text by Colin Sorensen and Mike Seaborne

# NISHEN

*Editorial Notice*

All the pictures shown in this book are from the collection of the Museum of London. The publisher would like to thank Mike Seaborne, Curator of the Museum's Historic Photographs Collection.
New prints for reproduction were made from copy negatives of the original prints. The pictures are reproduced by permission of the Reid Archive Collection.


The Photo-Library is being edited by Colin Osman and Dirk Nishen

Front Cover:
The entrance of Blackfriars Station. Built in the ›Moorish‹ style at the approach to Blackfriars Bridge, it stands on the site of what was once the bank of the River Fleet, a major tributary of the Thames, now enclosed. The now-familiar ›circle and bar‹ sign of London Transport, clearly seen here, was adopted for the city's unified transport system in 1933.


Back Cover:
Fish Street Hill, looking south towards Lower Thames Street. For centuries, this street was the northern approach to London Bridge, which crossed the River Thames just beyond the tower of the church of St Magnus the Martyr, visible in the distance. The great column, known to Londoners as ›The Monument‹, the base of which fills the centre of this view, commemorates the great Fire of London, which destroyed much of the City in 1666.

The publisher will be pleased to send further information on the titles available in his current programme, a selection of which you will find on the concluding page of this volume. Please send a postcard to the adress given below.


© 1987 Dirk Nishen Publishing, 19 Doughty Street, GB-London WC1N 2PT
Printed in Germany. All rights reserved.
Typesetting: Nishen/Lübecker Fotosatz, using the Walbaum Times type-face
Lithographs: O.R.T. Kirchner + Graser, D-Berlin
Printing: H.Heenemann, D-Berlin
Binding: H.Hensch, D-Berlin
The publisher wishes to thank all parties involved

ISBN 1 85378 102 9

# George Reid's views of Westminster and London

The photographs of George Reid are in the tradition of London view-makers. A major source of our knowledge about London in the 18th and 19th centuries comes from the work of the numerous topographical painters and draughtsmen who recorded the changing face of the ever-expanding city. A century before Reid was at work with his camera, similar views of London had been made by Thomas Shotter Boys, George Scharf and others.

The advent of photography provided a new method of making visual records, and its capacity for accurately rendering detail far surpassed even the finest efforts of artists using traditional media. Among the earliest of the photographs taken by William Henry Fox Talbot, inventor of photography in England, is a series of London views, including one of the unfinished Nelson Column, taken in 1845. Talbot had been quick to realise the value of photography in record-making, and topographical views form a large part of the body of photographs taken by him and his contemporaries.

Of the many topographical photographers who worked in London in the 19th century, one of the best was George Washington Wilson. In the 1880s he, together with his son Charles, produced a remarkable series of ›instantaneous‹ views of London streets. These photographs were taken from the inside of a covered horse-drawn van, hired for the purpose. The driver was instructed to pull-up at selected kerbside positions where Wilson waited, camera at the ready, for a suitable moment to make the exposure. One of the outstanding features of these photographs is the way in which passing traffic and people have been incorporated into the composition.

When we look at Reid's photographs we see that he too was particularly concerned to record the activities of the street as well as the streets and buildings themselves. The people of London and the visitors from the provinces and overseas animate these scenes, but it is the streets and squares – and the theatres, railway stations, churches, and other public buildings – that are the principal subjects and the main ›characters‹.

A further feature which Reid's approach shared with Wilson's was the choice of an elevated vantage point. However, rather than the platform of a horse-drawn van, Reid used a custom-built piece of apparatus resembling, when erected, a tall step-ladder, on top of which he mounted his camera. This provided an elevation of about 10 feet, and when the picture had been taken, the camera – a wooden whole-plate stand camera – could be removed and the apparatus folded up to form a sort of hand-cart which could then be pushed to the next location.

Working some 40 years after Wilson, Reid had, of course, access to much more sensitive and reliable photographic materials. He made good use of them, taking his pictures in widely different, and sometimes difficult, lighting conditions. Indeed, many of his photographs are outstanding for their pictorial qualities.

It is interesting to note that most of the scenes photographed by Reid serve as a reminder that three decades into this century, London appeared still a largely 19th century city. It is only when we look closely at the figures and the traffic that we realise that these photographs record London as it was in the late 1920s and early 1930s. To a contemporary Londoner, looking at Reid's photographs, it must come as a surprise to realise how much of the city's movement of goods and commodities was still horse-drawn. With the advantages of hindsight, it is distressing to realise how soon much of what we see here was to disappear, due either to the immense devastation of wartime bombing or through the redevelopments that have occured since the Second World War.

Reid would, however, have been aware that certain changes were already taking place. Britain during the 1920s and 1930s was in the grip of a deep economic depression and there were political and social forces at work which would have a lasting effect on British society. London, during this period remained relatively prosperous, its expanding population swelled by the arrival of thousands of newcomers from other parts of the country. Its public services, as well as its building industry, were developing quickly to meet the increased demands for new factories, offices, housing, public transport and other utilities. The ›modernist‹ architecture of the Hoover factory and Battersea Power Station, the suburbs of ›Metroland‹ and the new purpose-built cinemas for the ›talkies‹ were all created during this period, and a recognisably modern London was beginning to emerge.

Reid, however, seems to have chosen not to record these things, and it may be that like many of those who have set out to record the appearance of Britain's cities and countryside, he was concerned to commemorate that which was clearly about to pass. In his photographs, many clues to changes that were occuring, or were about to occur, to the character and appearance of London can be seen, but it is the streets and buildings of the past which fill the frames of Reid's photographs.

*Colin Sorensen/Mike Seaborne*

George Reid's photographic apparatus, shown extended ready for picture-taking (left) and folded-up for moving on to the next location (right).

The Forecourt at Victoria Station. This station was actually two separate buildings, built by rival railway companies each serving suburban London and the South of England. They were merged with other companies in 1923 to form the Southern Railway and the two stations were linked together. To the right of the station, and connected to it, stands the large Grosvenor Hotel.

A view across the River Thames from the steps of the Tate Gallery. Originally dedicated to British Art, the Tate was opened in 1897. Since for many years this gallery was considered to be situated inconveniently far from the centre of London, there was usually a good trade for taxi cabs, such as those seen waiting here.

Fleet Street, looking west. For more than two centuries, Fleet Street has been associated with newspaper production. Since it rises steeply from the now-covered course of the River Fleet, ascending the steep incline was a hard task for the wagon horses which, as late as the 1930s, pulled loads of huge rolls of paper from the docks to the newspaper printing works.

7

Fleet Street, looking west, with the church of St Dunstan's-in-the-West on the right. The tower of this church is thought to be the one which inspired Charles Dickens' Christmas story, ›The Chimes‹. The uniformed figure crossing the pavement in the foreground is one of a now-vanished ›race‹ of messenger boys who were once to be seen hurrying everywhere in central London.

The half-timbered gateway leading to the church of St Bartholomew-the-Great, one of London's oldest churches. It stands at one corner of Smithfield, a large open space, once a noted popular gathering place for occasions as various as fairs and public executions. It was also the site of a vast open-air cattle market, and is still the centre of London's meat trade.

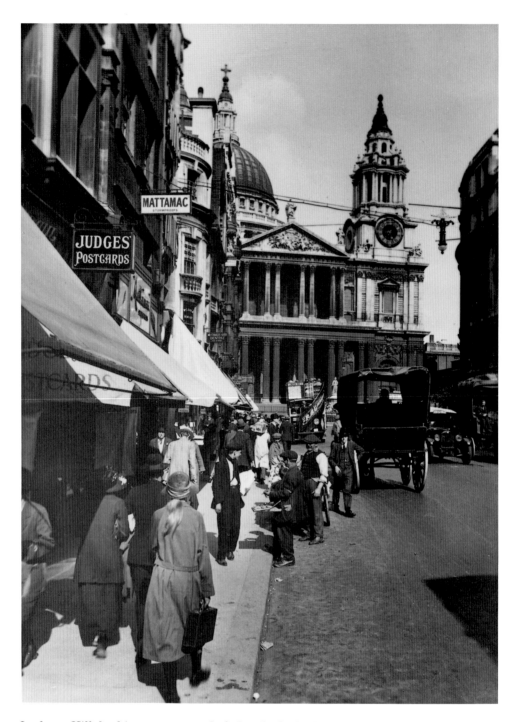

Ludgate Hill, looking east towards St Paul's Cathedral. Reid chose a characteristically elevated position for his version of one of the most photographed of London views. The density and speed of present-day traffic prevents such kerb-side trading as can be seen here.

Bow Lane. The junction with the ancient Roman road, Watling Street, forms the crossroads in the centre of this view. The ›Olde Watling‹ tavern was one of the first buildings to be erected after the Great Fire of London in 1666. It was followed a few years later by the church of St Mary Aldermary, designed by Sir Christopher Wren, the tower of which rises beyond.

The imposing front of what was, in Reid's time, the Kings Cross terminus of the London and North Eastern Railway. It was built to the designs of Lewis Cubitt, for the Great Northern Railway (predecessor of the LNER) in 1852. In 1867 the London terminus of the Midland Railway, St Pancras Station, was built alongside it. Both companies are now absorbed into British Rail.

The forecourt of the Southern Railway's terminus at London Bridge. This was the oldest railway terminus in London, having been built for the line linking London and Greenwich in 1836. The double-decked bus on the right belongs to the General Omnibus Company which was soon, in 1933, to become part of the London Transport system.

View of Whitehall from the garden in Parliament Square. The statue on the left is of the 19th century Statesman, Lord Palmerston. The gardens were remodelled after the Second World War and a statue of Sir Winston Churchill now stands on approximately this spot.

Whitehall, looking north. The buildings of the Home Office stand on the left. In the centre is the white shape of the Cenotaph, a monument to the dead service men and women of both world wars. Originally built, to a design of Sir Edwin Lutyens, in wood for the Victory Parade of 1919, it was replaced by the present stone version the following year as the result of a public campaign.

The floodlit front of Buckingham Palace. In the early 1900s, in addition to the building of a great memorial to Queen Victoria, a number of alterations and improvements were made to the palace and its approaches. Admiralty Arch was built, linking the Mall with Trafalgar Square, and the facade of the palace was refaced to a design by Sir Aston Webb.

Looking towards Coventry Street across Piccadilly Circus. The London Pavilion, in the centre of this view, was built as a music hall in the 1880s and later became a theatre and then a cinema. The lamps in the foreground mark the location of an underground public toilet, in its turn replaced by the circular concourse of the Piccadilly underground railway station.

The north side of Leicester Square, looking west. The Empire Theatre, on the left of the picture, once a famous music hall, was converted into a cinema shortly before this photograph was taken. In the centre, can be seen Daly's Theatre, which was demolished in 1937, and beyond it, the London Hippodrome.

Looking south across Trafalgar Square. The Nelson Column, one of London's most familiar landmarks, was still being built when it became the subject of one of the first photographs ever taken in London, by W.H.Fox Talbot in 1845. The lions at its base (sculpted by Sir Edwin Landseer) were installed in the 1870s.

Cranbourn Street, looking towards the London Hippodrome. This theatre was for long associated with the production of spectacular musical comedies. The figures of a charioteer and horses on the roof recall that the building was originally opened as a circus, in 1900.

Charing Cross Road. The Astoria Cinema, opened in 1927, can be seen on the left – on the opposite side of St Giles's Circus stands the even-larger cinema, The Dominion, Tottenham Court Road, built in 1929 on the site of Meux's Brewery – one of the ›sights‹ of London in the 19th century.

Charing Cross Road, looking north. On the right is the Garrick Theatre (opened in 1889), when, at the time of Reid's photograph, the young Laurence Olivier was playing a supporting role in ›The Stranger Within‹. To the left rises the oriental-style entrance of ›The Alhambra‹ music hall and beyond can be seen the facade of the London Hippodrome.

The North-Eastern corner of Trafalgar Square. In the foreground, a street trader displays animated dolls for sale on the steps of St Martin's-in-the-Fields church. The hotel building on the left was replaced by South Africa House in 1935.

The Strand, looking towards Trafalgar Square and the Nelson Column. On the left is an elaborately-dressed window of the Strand Corner House, one of the many popular restaurants owned by J.Lyons and Co. Ltd. which were then a feature of central and suburban London.

King William IV Street, viewed from the Strand and showing, on the left, one of the three architectural ›Pepper-pots‹ marking the corners of an early 19th century building which popular insistence, in the 1970s, saved from destruction. To the right is the bulk of Charing Cross Hospital, now largely demolished.

St Paul's Church, Covent Garden, designed by Inigo Jones and built in the 1630s. In the foreground are piled the boxes and baskets, then characteristic features of the Covent Garden Flower, Fruit and Vegetable Market. Beneath the portico of the church, the flower-seller Eliza Doolittle first encounters Prof. Higgins in Bernard Shaw's ›Pygmalion‹.

Long Acre. The tile-covered entrance of Covent Garden Station, seen here, is connected to the underground railway platforms by one of the deepest lift-shafts in central London. The difficulty of keeping road traffic moving in the vicinity of Covent Garden Market often necessitated, as here, the superintendence of a police constable.

Drury Lane, Covent Garden. Beyond the market porters and van drivers, refreshing themselves with mugs of tea, stands Drury Lane Theatre, which has been associated with many of the great names of the British theatre. These included the early 19th century actor, Edmund Kean, who was the subject of the biographical play being presented there at the time of the photograph.

The church of St Clement Danes, largely built to the designs of Sir Christopher Wren. Between the church and the memorial to the 19th century Prime Minister, W. E.Gladstone, left foreground, is one of the once-familiar granite water troughs provided by the Metropolitan Drinking Fountain & Cattle Trough Association for the refreshment of horses.

The Strand, looking east towards the church of St Clement Danes, with Australia House on the left. In the middle foreground, just beyond the fire alarm column and the large ›pillar box‹, for posting letters, an old man winds a street ›hurdy-gurdy‹ organ.

The Strand, looking east towards St Mary-le-Strand. This church was left on an is-
land in the midst of the traffic as the result of the building of the new streets of
Kingsway and Aldwych in the early 1900s. On the far left of the picture is Marconi
House, which was an early home of the BBC.

*George Reid*
*River Thames in the Twenties & Thirties*
Edited by Mike Seaborne
THE PHOTO-LIBRARY I, 32 pages, 30 pictures, £ 2.95


*Arthur Cross/Fred Tibbs*
*The London Blitz*
Edited by Mike Seaborne
THE PHOTO-LIBRARY III, 32 pages, 30 pictures, £ 2.95


*George Rodger*
*Magnum Opus*
Fifty Years in Photojournalism
Edited by Colin Osman
112 pages, 100 pictures, duotone printing, £ 12.95 (softcover), £ 19.95 (hardcover)


*Edith Tudor Hart*
*The Eye of Conscience*
THE PHOTO-POCKET-BOOK I, 128 pages, 115 pictures, £ 5.95


*Peter Keetman*
*A week at the Volkswagen factory*
Pictures from 1953
Edited by Rolf Sachsse
THE PHOTO-POCKET-BOOK II, 96 pages, 75 pictures, duotone printing, £ 5.95

**Dirk Nishen Publishing**
19 Doughty Street, GB – London WC1N 2PT, 01/2420185